I Pray for
My Friends

I Pray for My Friends
By Cara Barilla

ISBN 9780645285178

Copyright Cara Barilla 2024
All rights reserved 2024

Published by Little Lemon Book Co.
SYDNEY
www.littlelemonbookco.com.au

Written by Cara Barilla
www.authorcarabarilla.com.au
@AuthorCaraBarilla

Illustrated by Eleonora Cali
@Roxanne_Drawings

Layout by Jessica Chaplin
www.jesschaplincreative.com.au
@jesschaplincreative

This book is available in quantity for your group or organisation.
For more information please contact Little Lemon Book Co.

Printed in Australia.

For preschool and primary school age.

Little Lemon Book Co. First Edition 2024

I Pray for
My Friends

Written by Cara Barilla
Illustrated by Eleonora Cali

I pray for my friends who are cheerful

So bright, bubbly and loud

Smiling hearts are so beautiful

You grace us as you stand up proud

I pray for those
who may be feeling sad

It's ok if you're confused
or shy

Friends are here to help
and we're so glad

To be there for your comfort
as you try

I pray for those who are
strong like stone

Even if you don't reveal that
you're down

Please know that
you are never alone

Together we can
turn up your frown

I pray for those
who are here

You continue to fill
my heart always

I know you will always
be helpfully near

No matter the stretch
of our pathways

I pray for all of my friends' unique voices

You shed us daily with colour and light

We are here to have a guided choice

And will forever be cherished so tight

I pray for us to be safe together

Let us help others
safely and pray

As little acts of kindness last forever

As one simple smile can
brighten up one's day

I pray for those who may
feel a mess

Or who have a long
way to endure

We will share a hug and
prayers to bless

Simple prayers are forever alight
and pure

I pray for families who are coming and going

Even if we don't meet again for sure

I pray through my heart without your knowing

Guiding you safely upon your new adventures

I pray for all the friends all over this earth

To help, heal, be kind, be gentle and pray

If I never see you again, for all that its worth

You have kindly brightened up my day!

Amen.

About the Author

Cara Barilla is a proud mother of two children
and resides in Sydney, Australia.

As an experienced writer and educator, she continues to
use her passion of helping others through art and literature
to find a piece of their happiness and one's connection of
'self love' through the powerful message of words.

Cara has a strong passion for art, creative writing, poetry,
wellness and continues to inspire and assist people of all
walks of life through her art of creativity.

www.ingramcontent.com/pod-product-compliance
Lightning Source LLC
Chambersburg PA
CBHW040253100426

42811CB00011B/1247